**CCSS Genre** Fable

YO-AEX-240

**Essential Question**
What can animals in stories teach us?

# The Dog
## and the Bone

by Ann Weil
illustrated by Bob Dacey

# CHAPTER 1

# Lucky Day!

It was a warm, sunny day. Dog felt lucky. He stuck his nose in a pile of leaves. Dog felt something.

He said, "I believe it is a bone." He pushed away the colorful leaves with his nose.

Dog was right. It was a bone.

leaves

Dog was fond of bones. He liked big bones best, and this bone was huge!

Dog said, "Today is my lucky day!" He picked up the bone.

bone

STOP AND CHECK

Why does Dog think it is his lucky day?

# CHAPTER 2

# A New Way Home

Then Dog saw some other <u>dogs</u>. The other dogs were watching him. They looked hungry. They wanted his bone.

| Language Detective | <u>Dogs</u> is a plural noun. Find another plural noun on page 4. |
|---|---|

Dog did not want to fight. He decided to take his bone home. He would lie in the sun and feast on it there.

But Dog was far from home. He decided to try a new way to get home. Maybe it would be faster.

Dog ran through fields and past trees and houses. He saw a cat on a fence but decided not to chase it.

Dog walked and walked until he came to a brook. The water looked cold and deep. Dog did not like to swim, so he looked for a way to cross. He saw a log bridge.

Dog said, "I think I can cross that old bridge."

brook

log bridge

STOP AND CHECK

What has Dog done so far in this story?

# CHAPTER 3

# A Better Bone?

Dog stepped onto the bridge. It felt solid. Still, Dog was careful. He watched where he put his feet.

Dog looked down. He saw something remarkable in the water.

| **Language Detective** | Stepped onto the bridge is the predicate in this sentence. Find another predicate on this page. |
| --- | --- |

Dog saw another dog. The other dog was looking at him, and he had a big bone, too. Dog could not take his eyes off the other bone. It looked bigger and more delicious than Dog's bone.

**In Other Words** kept looking at. En español: *no podía dejar de mirar.*

Dog said, "I must have that bone!"
He tried to snatch the bone away
from the other dog. But then Dog's
bone fell out of his mouth! It made
a huge splash and then sank under
the water.

splash

Dog did not expect that to happen. But Dog did not care that he had lost his bone. He would get the other, bigger bone instead.

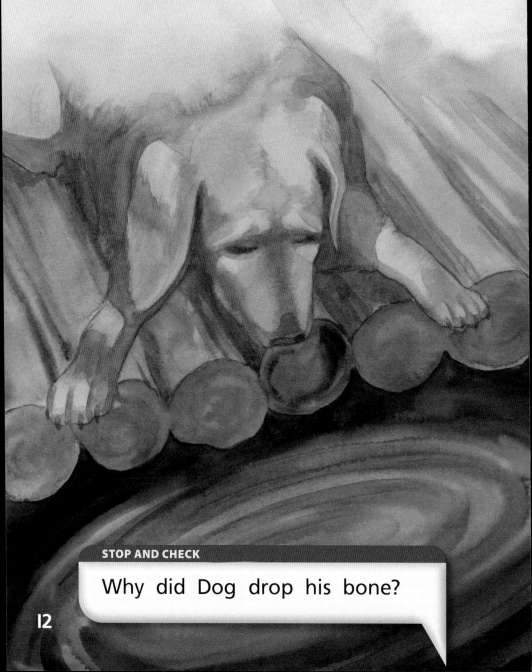

**STOP AND CHECK**

Why did Dog drop his bone?

CHAPTER 4

# A Lesson Learned

But the other dog was no longer there. Dog looked for the bone. The bone was gone, too.

Where was it now?

Dog had lost his bone. Now he had nothing. Dog felt sad as he walked home. It was not his lucky day.

Fables are stories with lessons.
The lesson is called a moral.
Here is the moral of this fable:

Greed can lead us to lose what we already have.

**STOP AND CHECK**

What lesson did Dog learn?

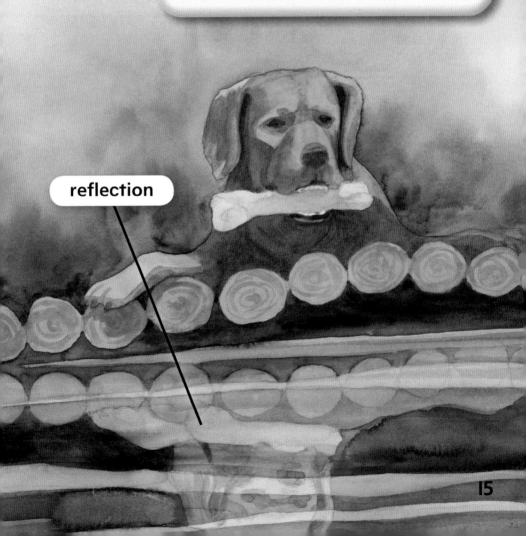

reflection

# Respond to Reading

## Summarize

Use important details to summarize *The Dog and the Bone.* The chart may help.

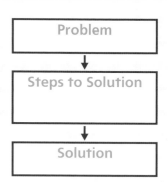

## Text Evidence

1. How do you know that *The Dog and the Bone* is a fable? Genre

2. What is Dog's problem at the beginning of the story? Problem and Solution

3. Use your knowedge of suffixes to figure out the meaning of *careful* on page 9. Suffixes

4. Write about why Dog lost his bone. Write About Reading

**Compare Texts**
Read another animal story that can teach a lesson.

# The Dingo
## and His Shadow

meat

Dingo had some meat. He saw a black dog next to him. The black dog had meat, too.

Dingo said, "Two pieces of meat are better than one." Dingo tried to grab the black dog's meat.

17

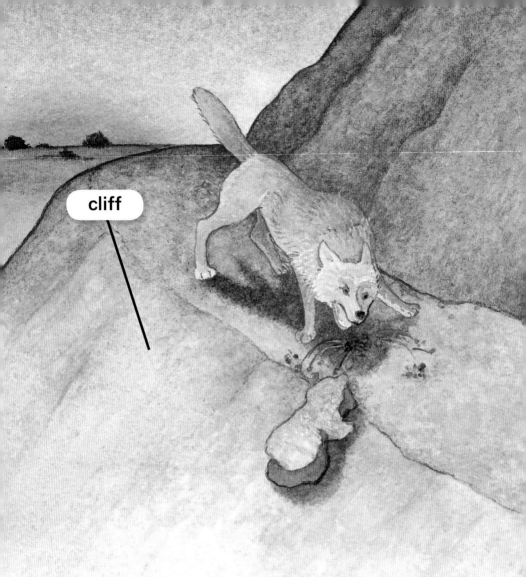

cliff

Dingo's meat fell from his mouth and tumbled off the cliff.

Dingo thought he would get the black dog's meat. Instead, he got a mouthful of dirt.

18

The other dog was only a shadow.

The moral of this story is: When you grasp at the shadow, you lose the real thing.

kangaroo

## Make Connections

What do these two animal stories teach us? Essential Question

How is Dingo like Dog? Text to Text

**Dialogue** Dialogue is what the characters in a story say.

**What to Look For** As you read, look for quotation marks: " ". They show where dialogue begins and ends. Look at this example:

Dog said, "I think I can cross that old bridge."

**Your Turn**

Write a short animal story. Put dialogue in the story. Use quotation marks around the words each character says.

20

# Thinkmark

## Setting

Where does *The Dog and the Bone* take place?

## Characters

Who is the main character in *The Dog and the Bone?*

## Sequence of Events

What happens in this story?

What is Dog's problem? Why does Dog lose his bone?

## Make Connections

How is *The Dog and the Bone* like other stories you have read?

# Animals in Stories

## GR J • Benchmark 18 • Lexile 320

Grade 2 • Unit 2 Week 2

**www.mheonline.com**

The **McGraw·Hill** Companies

ISBN-13 978-0-02-118877-2
MHID 0-02-118877-7

99701

EAN

9 780021 188772

2

**Mc Graw Hill** Education

# Uncle Ned's Cabin
## and the Lost Cause

By M.B. Barnes and
Transcribed by Charles W. Locklin